The Door on Every Tear

The Door on Every Tear

Poems

Neil Carpathios

RESOURCE *Publications* • Eugene, Oregon

THE DOOR ON EVERY TEAR
Poems

Copyright © 2020 Neil Carpathios. All rights reserved. Except for brief quotations in critical publications or reviews, no part of this book may be reproduced in any manner without prior written permission from the publisher. Write: Permissions, Wipf and Stock Publishers, 199 W. 8th Ave., Suite 3, Eugene, OR 97401.

Resource Publications
An Imprint of Wipf and Stock Publishers
199 W. 8th Ave., Suite 3
Eugene, OR 97401

www.wipfandstock.com

PAPERBACK ISBN: 978-1-7252-5740-5
HARDCOVER ISBN: 978-1-7252-5741-2
EBOOK ISBN: 978-1-7252-5742-9

Manufactured in the U.S.A.   01/06/20

For my sister and brother

Contents

I. From Inside

From Inside | 3
Now That You're Here | 4
In the Middle of a Day like Any Other | 6
What Happens Under the Overpass | 8
Back Page, Front Page | 9
"Pain Is Weakness Leaving the Body" | 11
Life Sucks | 13
Regulars | 15
Morning Rescued from the Banal | 16
Flea Market | 18
Cocoon | 19
Janitor | 21
Paying Attention | 22
"What Is Truly More Moving than Beauty Is Its Ruin" | 23
When the Waitress Is Not Friendly | 25
Choosing | 26
The Statue and Us | 27

II. The Function of Sadness

The Function of Sadness | 31
Spilled Milk | 32
Choose Your Own Adventure | 33
In the Middle of the Night | 34
What I Overheard on the Last Day: Two Angels Hovering in a Corner | 36
The Spare Self | 37
Angels Waving Hello, Goodbye? | 38
Picking a Casket | 39
Don't Worry | 40

The Museum of All the Places We've Made Love | 41

At Eighty-Five | 42

Focus | 43

Sure | 44

I Don't Know What to Call This | 45

Breath of Venus | 46

My Father at 3 AM | 47

Her Wind Chimes | 48

Two Years Later | 49

III. The Afterlife

The Afterlife | 53

Between the Appetizers and the Entrees | 54

Urgent Prayer | 55

The Stain on the Concrete | 56

The Woodpecker | 57

Self-Service | 59

Squid | 60

Treasures | 62

Stethoscope | 63

My Wife Taking Off Her Shirt | 65

Stethoscope II | 67

Grandson | 68

The Dream | 69

Watching TV With Brodie | 70

Random Love | 71

Love Account | 72

Why I Like the Wind | 74

Bargain | 76

I Enter the Door | 77

Acknowledgments

Grateful acknowledgment is made to the following publications in which these poems first appeared:

Braided Way: "Cocoon," "Random Love"

Chiron Review: "Regulars"

Confrontation: "What Is Truly More Moving than Beauty Is its Ruin"

Echo Literary Journal: "Life Sucks"

I-70 Review: "The Afterlife"

Linden Avenue Review: "Pain Is Weakness Leaving the Body"

Maximum Tilt: "Why I Like the Wind"

Orson's Review: "Between the Appetizers and the Entrees," "Urgent Prayer," "The Stain on the Concrete," "The Woodpecker"

Right Hand Pointing: "In the Middle of a Day like Any Other"

SO IT GOES Literary Journal: "What Happens Under the Overpass"

Soul-Lit: "Flea Market," "When the Waitress Is Not Friendly"

The Windhover: "Paying Attention"

The Write Room: "The Function of Sadness"

"What Happens Under the Overpass" appeared in *Not Far from Me: Stories of Opioids and Ohio* (Ohio State University Press, 2019).

"The Afterlife" appeared in *The Doll Collection* (Terrapin Books, 2016).

"Back Page, Front Page" appeared in *Veils, Halos and Shackles: International Poetry on the Abuse and Oppression of Women* (Kasva Press, 2016).

The following poems appeared in *The Function of Sadness* (winner of the 2015 Slipstream Press Chapbook Award): "Now That You're Here," "In the Middle of a Day like Any Other," "What Happens Under the Overpass," "Pain Is Weakness Leaving the Body," "The Statue and Us," "The Function of Sadness," "Cocoon," "The Afterlife," and "Choosing."

I.
From Inside

From Inside

On every teardrop

there is a door
we can enter.

From inside,
through the glassy walls

as the tear falls
we see what we thought we knew,

magnified.

Now That You're Here

                        you may as well join me
as I use a hose to water concrete
of my driveway as if it might grow,
pretending not to spy
on their strange conversation—
my neighbor's son, whose face was torn off
in a motorcycle accident, talking with his hands
to his father, whose arms were blown off
in a factory mishap.
The father smiles.
His gold front tooth shines.
Judging by the father's eyes,
the boy's eyes may have been blue,
spilling over like water.
They talk a long time,
one with words, the other
with gestures.

                We can watch the first firefly
blink. The son points
as if he can see through
the mask of skin
with no openings.
In the front yard they stand
encircled by more and more
fireflies, penumbra of energy
pulsing. Behind them
on the porch
a little girl wearing an eye patch
reads.

            From the assembly-line of moments
making up a day
we might notice the sound of water

licking pavement
and the sky's egg cracking open
spilling out stars.
We can flush ants from between
the cracks.
We can spray figure eights.
We can stall long enough,
not knowing exactly why,
to witness something
at the furthest edge
of something else
until the girl's flashlight dies,
although she doesn't move
from her spot,
and the two men keep talking
even after all of them
have disappeared.

In the Middle of a Day like Any Other

      Next to the abandoned
shoe lace factory
    with windows boarded up,
the hookers and pimps,
      the addicts and war vets
in electric wheelchairs
    ornament the walk.

At a red light
    I'm stopped,
and suddenly think
      this is like reading
a poem
    by a great poet,
say Stevens or Blake,
      pretending I wrote it
myself,
    which is what happens
when atoms we're made of
      that once were part
of the stars
    all sizzle at once.

A woman with dreadlocks,
      mumbling, pushes a cart
full of god-knows-what.
    A man in a torn sweatshirt
drags one leg
      like his pet on a leash.
The woman points,
    says something.
The man answers.

        She reaches into her junk,
pulls out a plastic flower,
        stem and all,
hands it to him
        the way a child would
and he bows his head
        in thanks.

The red light ends
        but the poem hasn't,
so I linger
        as they shuffle past—
shoulders brushing,
        in opposite directions,
she mumbling again,
        he pulling
the attached dead part
        of himself—

both unaware
        that they are glowing
from something
        inside them
flaring,
        like fireflies
in a jar.

What Happens Under the Overpass

My friend who lived homeless for a year
tells me. You masturbate with your hand
or sometimes a cement pillar. You pick
lice out of your hair and pretend
they're licetronauts you flick
into orbit. You use an empty bottle
to shatter the skull of someone
who says suck me or else.
You urinate and watch the steam
cloud mushroom like a ghost.
You listen to cars and trucks
voom by above you like huge
metallic gods. You find a half-
eaten Twinkee with ants dotting
the cream and you eat it,
licking your fingers. You read
the graffiti, add a few pearls
of your own with a broken Bic.
You use a newspaper for a blanket.
You pick scabs on your legs
and create smeared jelly blood art.
You study the clouds shifting
as if they are symbols on a treasure
map. You hum to drown out
your stomach's growling. You stare
down at your hands that are swollen
and empty and holding nothing,
the way you entered the world.

Back Page, Front Page

On the back page of the paper
the story of a girl
who can't feel pain,
who might at first glance
be a superhero,
her face emotionless
as she steps on a nail.
What the government wouldn't do
for an army like her,
perishable yes,
but marching into danger,
fearless.
She's not been trained
like some elite warrior
who endures tortures—

she's ten with a disorder
that affects
how pain travels
to the brain,
one of just one hundred humans worldwide.
She never cried
with diaper rash
though she almost died
from appendicitis
due to no warnings.

What if she switched
with the girl on the front page,
twelve years old,
finally found after missing
two years
chained in the basement
of a deranged neighbor,

kept as his sex slave,
who told police
the man shoved things
way up inside her—
bottles, sticks, a live rat—
and carved into her belly
his name with a straightened hanger,
glowing hot,
claimed he actually loved her
in his own way
and told her,
"I'm making you into Wonder Woman
who can take anything."

Some coincidence—or is it?—
like two sides
of the same coin
on the same day
meant for us to neatly file
somewhere in memory.
And the way the articles end
as if the two girls
for a sick joke
had consulted,
the one on the back
who regularly attends
a camp called *Painless But Hopeful,*
the one on the front
who can't remember
or refuses to say
her own name
as if that person is dead,
when asked what is the secret
of survival, answers
"You have to learn not to feel things
too much anymore."

"Pain Is Weakness Leaving the Body"

      I read on the back of the kid's shirt,
given to him
by the marine recruiter.

      But I've never seen it leave,
even when my father's bone tore through
his shin and he screamed, almost operatic,
in the yard.

      Or when
Jimmy Galloway chopped his thumb off
in woodshop and blood
shot out
and we stood, our mouths agape.

      Or my own
sprained ankles,
colonoscopy,
cracked ribs.

      Is it a perfect replica,
a body within our body,
pushing like a chick
till it hatches,
invisible, like a ghost?

      Does it fly to the moon?
      Does it swan dive into grass?
      Does it seek other weakness
to join hands and dance?

        I wonder if the saying rises
from memory, in a kid who wore the shirt
proudly, if it helps as he squirms
on dirt, his chest ripped open by a bomb,

            his one eye searching the sky
for weakness leaving his body
as his other eye rolls away like a marble?

Life Sucks

Somebody wants us to see
    so badly he printed the words
with letters four feet high
    in purple spray paint

on the brick wall by the freeway.
    He risked getting caught.
It was important to get the message out,
    to remind us the cold, hard fact.

When he drives by does he feel proud?
    Does he think: *I've done my part,*
added my two cents?
    Does he nudge his girl beside him in the car—

"See that, I did that!"—
    and she coos at his bold,
understated, masterful
    summarization of modern life?

He must have forgot—
    the way we do—
when he
    slithered free

from womb-jail
    into a nest
of arms,
    life's first safety net,

and the brilliant light
    and the blinking hard.
It all ends soon enough, doesn't it?
    True, a visitor from outer space

spying from a hidden vantage place
    would probably guess we're light years
from bliss.
    But he might also spot behind that wall
the dogwood flowering
    with a bird in it,
and the little girl on the sidewalk
    chasing a butterfly,

her flip-flops slapping,
    her giggling a new strange something
he can't quite name
    though he'd like to take it back with him

for dissection and analysis.
    Somebody wants us to know
just how bad it is.
    World we inherit, almost by accident,

this little while.
    Two huge purple words,
shrinking,
    in my rearview mirror.

Regulars

We sit at the counter, same spots, as if rumps need same stools to feel loved. One of us slurps coffee in the usual key, one of us tells the dumb knock-knock, one of us never looks up from a crossword. We're a family, at least every Monday- Wednesday-Friday morning before my eight o'clock class, something to kick-start the hours even if it annoys like Raspy (what he's been baptized by Demetri the cook) hacking in the corner from his three packs-a-day, killing appetites. And the one called Vegas (nobody knows his real name)—an unlit cigar always in his mouth—waits for his eggs, same scrambled, drizzled with hot sauce, wheat toast, tea, but today he keeps scratching his bald head with a match as if trying to set it on fire, not reading the sports, for once not bitching about the Browns. What's wrong? Did the way the hostess stonewalled his flirting with conviction make him miss his former self, black gelled hair like polished rock, cheekbone skin taut, no belly, biceps popping? Does he try to locate his long-lost skill to navigate the confidence-destroyingly beautiful fact of a woman's face? Does the match's friction spark heroic lucidity, at least some consolation? His plate arrives, but he doesn't notice, he's looking up at the ceiling's universe adrift somewhere, still going at it—calculating losses? conjuring lottery picks? wondering if when we die is the darkness gentle?—working on a terrible itch or thinking hard, maybe for us, like a saint, as the eggs get cold, all of us getting older, soon to exit into our separate worlds but for a while still here, connected by bacon fat, griddle hiss and time's mysterious hold on us, and finally he returns to Earth, to Ohio, to this diner and stares down into his mug as the teabag leaks its copper blood.

Morning Rescued from the Banal

Thank you, aproned woman
behind the counter
who stops slicing a lemon
into yellow wheels

for a mouse's carriage
to look out the big front window
with the rest of us.
Thank you, other waitress

also watching
who drops the phone
like it bit your ear
letting it plunge

like a bungee jumper
on a cord and you gasp
as if it is a baby
nearly hitting the floor.

Thank you, old geezer
slurping a bowl of green soup,
your fake teeth resting
on top of a stick of butter,

who looks up, becoming
a statue, the spoon
suspended near your lips
not spilling a drop.

And thank you, most of all,
bizarro man channeling Blake,
who wrote, "Those who restrain desire
do because theirs is weak enough

to be restrained," the way you
hump a parking meter
in plain sight
and when the policeman

arrives to drag you away,
you wrap your arms around
the metal pole
and hold tighter.

Flea Market

I don't come to examine the used casting reels but to listen to the old man with a gold front tooth and sagging bicep tattoo heart with an arrow through it mythologize the bass and catfish he's expertly caught, and I don't come for the stuffed squirrel with an acorn in its small frozen claws on a wooden base but to let the same old man explain how a squirrel's sense of balance is unmatched which is why they don't fall tight-roping a telephone line or leaping like acrobats branch to branch. I don't come for the fancy hubcaps or some grandchild's old tennis trophy or the whale bone necklace that once belonged to a grandmother who could forecast the weather. I come to see the woman with a hook for a hand trying to skewer flies in mid-air while telling about the necklace. I come to hear the little boy strumming a beat-up banjo with a top hat at his feet for donations. And mostly I come for the dreadlocked hillbilly hipster and his table covered with empty jars he claims hold God's laughs he caught like fireflies—just five dollars—one even now perched on my shoulder, he says.

Cocoon

How better to snicker
at vanity
than to stall
at a grocery checkout,
not moving,
remembering once reading
the average human spends
one hour a day waiting,
which is almost three years
in a lifetime,
and even though you see
at the front of the line
a woman sorting coins,
old, mumbling,
with holes in her sweater,
you feel aggravation
like a sewing machine
in your chest
working its thread,
spinning a cocoon
surrounding, separating
you from everyone—

then, finally,
she drops coins
into the clerk's open hand,
he counts,
but gives some back
and says
"Keep enough for bus fare,"
as if you were placed

exactly here,
this moment,
to witness the woman's
toothless grin,
the clerk's soft eyes,
to feel something stir
like wings inside unfolding.

Janitor

The old man sweeping the floor seems to be dancing. His partner, the broom, follows his lead, circles with him as he turns, tips, sways in a kind of waltz the length of the hallway abandoned now at nine o'clock, students and professors long gone at home sipping drinks, watching TV, maybe even loving another body in a cool, dark room. He whistles as his hips draw closer to the long broom's handle as if she's ready now to be whispered to in her ear, something tender, the way he once did with the girl that would become his wife, that would leave him one day too soon because of tumors in her chest. Samuel sees me beside the elevator— "What are you still doing here, prof?"— "Catching up grading," I say. Which ruins the dance, scaring her off. I wave, he waves back then returns to sweeping but without music and without her, which he's used to since she drifts in and out of his days unannounced and is shy around everybody but him the way she always was—he once confided leaning on that same broom, smoking a cigarette at the edge of the faculty lot. I look over my shoulder one more time, his broad back to me, the broom in his big hands, bristles *shooshing* back and forth on the floor's surface so steady, quiet, if it were a human voice it would be a whisper.

Paying Attention

You have to pay every morning before rising out of bed.
So you can hear the sound of the house when the house is sleeping,

and notice an ant crossing carpet dragging a tiny suitcase
full of tears. So you can look out the window and spy, next door,

your neighbor's roses whose poor, enormous heads bend,
praying. You have to drop coins into the slot of the invisible.

So you can read between each entry in the dictionary
other words that have always been there, pre-print,

before language. So you can see parentheses between people,
that hold thoughts, even though they feel separate, detached.

You have to save all your change for this, it's worth the cost,
passing a tramp crucified in his clothes,

yelling at no-one, and noticing an angel ignoring him—
arms crossed, rolling his eyes—then reaching out,

arms extended needing a hug, begging to be forgiven.
If attention demands more, find a way. Take out a loan,

get a second job to pay. So when you pull out of the lot
you can pause by the dumpster to see a crone

picking through garbage, loading a cart with kisses.
So later at the park you'll be in the right spot to see

Jesus—I swear—letting children stick index fingers
through holes in his palms. So on your way home you can pass

the same tramp shuffling, mumbling, on the corner and know
it's God Himself in shabby clothes talking to anyone who will listen.

"What Is Truly More Moving than Beauty Is Its Ruin"

—Rodin

Rainbows and sunsets,
waterfalls and mountains
are easy to admire.
And the stars at night.
And the blemishless,
airbrushed people
on covers of magazines.
Not the two grungy teens
on the sidewalk
comparing scars or tattoos—
fuck this, fuck that,
cunt, bitch, dickhead,
damn girl—
unspooling from their tongues
like venom,
cigarettes dangling
from pierced lips.
Not the grizzled men
sprouting like weeds
from concrete
holding cardboard signs.
But once I saw
such men
beneath a bridge in Pittsburgh
propping up a Charlie Brown tree
on Christmas Eve,
wrapping it with Caution tape,
sticking an empty Coke bottle
on top
for an angel or a star.
And if you slow down
long enough

and watch,
you might notice
above those grunge girls
in front of the 7-Eleven,
the cigarette smoke
haloing their weary heads.

When the Waitress Is Not Friendly

When the waitress is not friendly,
when the waitress is downright cold,
picture her in the dirty apartment
she barely can afford,
voices through her plaster wall
cursing, sounds of breaking glass,
as she tosses and finally sleeps,
drool leaking from the corner of
her mouth. Imagine being a fly
on her couch, watching her nervous
habit of chewing her nails, the way
she plays solitaire for hours alone
Saturday nights, chain-smoking,
drinking cheap wine. See her
mending holes in her socks
and plucking gray hairs from
her temples. Study her pained
expression when she looks at
her flabby naked body
in the mirror.
Peek behind her mask
that hides a little girl
who skinned her knee once,
with a bottom lip like yours
that quivered in embarrassment
and pain.
Feel the waitress' fingertips
as she frowns, her skin touching
yours, the brief second
that if some god pressed *Pause*
on his remote would freeze
your energy to hers
as she places the cool
metal spoon you asked for
onto your palm.

Choosing

    The TV was vomiting
dead babies,
        so I turned him off.
Then the newspaper arrived

    and proceeded to bleed
on my fingers,
        so I stuffed her in the trash.
The radio ranted

    about hellfire
and where we all were headed.
        I kindly disagreed.
The rest of the morning

    I welcomed dirty dishes
in the sink
        and warm suds on my hands.
I folded laundry

    and didn't mind
the missing sock, hiding,
        spying like a child.
I even relished bending

    to pick up sticks,
over and over,
        in the yard,
a kind of sanity,

    as a bird
with a cathedral in his throat
        high above everything
chose to sing.

The Statue and Us

The corners of the statue's eyes
were perfectly shaped
for tiny, almost microscopic bugs
to perch and have sex
and secrete,

so the tears that fell
down the stone cheeks
were hailed a miracle.

The people thought the statue
wept for them,
or was holy,

they traveled many miles
to come witness,
to maybe understand
the origin of all tears.
Meanwhile,

the real tears
everywhere all around them
continued. Of course they knew it.

But those were human tears.

II.

The Function of Sadness

The Function of Sadness

The face was designed to adjust
to loss. We were given eyelashes
to stitch the lids shut.

Trapped tears
turn into butterflies
that nest in the stomach.

When we're nervous
they wake up, flutter about,
which reminds us

we're not dead yet.

Spilled Milk

Who would cry over it?

    I picture an old widow, living alone.
She is tiny but round.
    Keeps the phone by her

    in case her children call. Which is rare.
There are pictures of Greek saints on the wall.
    She watches reruns of *Murder She Wrote,*

    reads the church bulletin. Uses a cane.
Ramps have been installed.
    She is brought home by a shuttle

    service from dialysis.
It could be worse.
    She falls asleep in her chair.

    In the kitchen she makes real coffee
once a week, her little reward. Sneaks
    a nibble of forbidden chocolate. Pours

    some skim milk for her coffee
but it sloshes onto the counter.
    She just stares at it—through it—

    for some reason, frozen there.
It happens like this
    when you'd least expect it.

Choose Your Own Adventure

In the book, the reader is the protagonist and has to pick a path. One option is to turn to the next page, the other is to skip several pages ahead to another destiny. My father comes on a ship from Greece. There are two job offers—one in Boston, the other in Canton, Ohio. The next page is Boston. Ohio starts on page ten. Why he chooses Ohio I don't know. Maybe because the word *hi* is in the name making it seem friendlier. Maybe because *can* is in Canton, boosting his confidence. But what if? He would never have met my mother but some New England woman on page two. Maybe his sperm would still have started me, but inside her. When I got a cold she'd have fed me clam chowder. I would have been forced to visit lots of boring museums—about the Tea Party, Paul Revere, and Ben Franklin's inventions. I'd have been a Red Sox fan and Larry Bird would have been a household name. I'd have hung out at Dunkin Donuts after school. I wouldn't pronounce my *r*'s and I'd "pak the ca in the yad" and pick up "gils at Havad Squae." But I am now on page fifty. In Ohio. Like a relay race, my father passed me the baton just before he died on page forty, so now I'm the protagonist. My Ohio mother is dying and I'm trying to spoon feed her rice pudding. Her arms are blue-black from nurses unable to locate veins. I can turn to the next page or skip several pages ahead. The only rule of the book is you aren't allowed to turn back.

In the Middle of the Night

        in the hospital
near the end
in her delirium,

I'm her father.

        She speaks Greek,
asks if I still squeeze lemons
into my soup.

Two hours later,

        I'm her husband,
my Dad.
She wants to know why

I look so tired,

        tells me not to worry,
says how badly she misses
my strong hands.

Even later,

        near sunrise,
she looks into my eyes,
searching, as if they might

give my name.

She knows she doesn't know.
I smile. She tries to.
Then she puts a hand on my cheek

and says

　　　"I don't know who you are,
but I know
that I love you."

What I Overheard on the Last Day: Two Angels Hovering in a Corner

"Took you long enough to get here. You didn't miss much.
Nothing too unusual. Eighty-seven, complications.
Hands and arms bruised black from needles over and over.
Opening in her chest where the pacemaker was planted—
pacemaker that wasn't keeping pace so a repairman came
to bend over her squirming body and adjust a wire, like fixing
a TV. Neck and chin purple from nurses tug-twisting to jam
the breathing tube down her throat. They all die. Everybody knows.
Sure, the way she glows yellow, jaundiced, is strange. Liver failure,
the doctor said. Pale carrot. Ripe banana. Weirdly angelic,
wouldn't you agree? Dialysis, yet again, was needed, regardless.
Nothing spectacular on the spectrum of exits. A room full of machines
whistling, beeping. Tubes sprouting from her, stains on sheets.
Her white hair wild. No weaponry, earthquakes, falling off cliffs.
Just a small woman on a bed. Somebody's mother. Somebody's yia yia.
Her hands in sock-mitts to stop her from pulling the plastic snake
gagging her. Happens every day, especially there.
Usually born in a hospital, usually die in one. Him, the oldest son,
was asked to hold her down while they plunged a needle
in her neck. Now he helps to tie her wrists to bed rails for her own good.
As death goes, no fireworks. Just the final morphine drips. Her breathing
shallow, blood pressure dropping. See how the daughter squeezes
her hand? See how the forehead chills the other son's lips? Fairly typical.
It was her time to go, people will say, she lived a long life, everybody's
time will come. Yes. Yes. Of course. The best part is about to begin.
You got here in time for that. The studying of the face, finally peaceful,
on the pillow. The way they curl up on chairs, and pace. The way the quiet
in the room is the opposite of a standing ovation or parade, but if you
really listen you can hear a kind of sad music, barely audible, coming through
their flesh. Rising from somewhere inside their shells while they wait."

The Spare Self

Like a spare tire,
    I feel safe knowing it's there,
        locked behind
            the cage of my ribs.

        In her hospital room
      they disconnected all the wires
    and tubes, said she'd be floating
away soon, as if she were a helium balloon

we'd let go of. My brother, my sister, my wife,
    the nurses—none of them noticed
        how I pulled it out while we looked,
            from the monitors going blank,

        to her face.
    Sometimes the self needs a break.
  It was a rabbit's foot, a lucky coin.
When her body was just a lump we touched

and stroked and kissed one last time,
    it did its job while my other self watched
        from the corner. It guided me to reach
            out for her hand and remember

            all the times as a boy crossing streets
        when she'd squeeze my hand, hard,
    making sure we stayed connected.
And I squeezed tight, there in the final

moments, trying to help her cross
    to the other side,
        safely, of wherever it was
            she was going.

Angels Waving Hello, Goodbye?

Moments after the machinery said
she died a nurse lifted her eyelids,
one at a time, and with a small flashlight,
looked into her eyes. I suppose,
to make sure. I looked, too,
at the brown pupils,
which reminded me of my daughter's
shortly after she was born—ironically,
so alive—the way they both seemed
to be staring, glazed but focused,
at something just outside of the scene
the rest of us couldn't see.

Picking a Casket

If she had come along to pick her own casket,
    would she have unleashed her quiet humor?

    Would she have asked the undertaker for a sporty model?
Maybe something in emerald green or fire engine red?

Or one that gets better mileage,
    given the long journey ahead?

    Would she have instructed my brother
and sister to distract him long enough so I could

give her a boost up into one on display
    for her to take on a test drive?

    Would she have commented on the new casket smell?
The plush interior? The cup holder big enough for

a jumbo coffee-to-go? Would she have apologized
    for taking so long to choose, saying that it's such a big

    decision and "won't it depreciate by as much as 15 percent
of its value the second we drive it off the lot?"

Don't Worry

The undertaker apologizes.
The concealer can only do so much.
"She was quite yellow, you know."
"Yes, we know. You did your best."

A final cruelty. This woman who wore
pearls and did her hair
just to go to the grocery
or drug store. Here she lies for all

to see, by her standards, a mess.
She didn't sense, from the room's corner
where they told me to wait, I spied—
as nurses changed her—her loose skin

hanging, maps of bruises,
breasts like deflated balloons,
the totality of the body I emerged from
come to this, a worn-out coat beyond

patching up. She complained, joking,
I never wrote poems about her.
What would she think of these words
immortalizing dishevelment?

Don't worry, Mom, we gave them your
favorite earrings to put on you,
we gave them the gray blouse
you instructed us to give. Don't worry,

sacred vessel I owe my life to
in this life we call *Mother*,
hardly anybody reads poems these days,
hardly anybody ever reads my poems.

The Museum of All the Places We've Made Love

It is not open to the public.
    I stroll through now and then,
admiring displays. Thousands.
    Each includes a video (edited for time purposes),

    more added daily.
Here, in my car next to the lake.
    There, the beach at dawn in Cozumel.
Bathtub. Porch swing. Sleeping bag.

Every room we've lived in.
    They are not arranged chronologically
or alphabetically. But I can tell which
    are older or more recent

    by the way we look. Now a new one,
roped off, about to be unveiled.
    I wait until the video begins . . .
Right after the funeral. Finally home,

the power strangely went out.
    We lit candles, drank wine, held each other.
There were no tears left, they were butterflies
    inside us. Then the lights came back on,

    but only after we were done.
As if my mother wanted
    to remind us
why we live at all.

At Eighty-Five

When I'd drop by I'd find her listening to country music or watching the country music channel on TV or leafing through country music magazines. She used to poke fun at the silly lyrics about guzzling beer and beat-up trucks and denim-clad mamas wearing cowboy boots. She used to mock the twangy tones, the banjos, the backwoods yodeling, her biggest target Garth Brooks. So why, I asked, suddenly all this country? She said "The only way is to immerse yourself, dive in, work through it like breaking in stiff jeans. Eventually, you get inside the thing's skin, you learn its heartbeat, you see the distance between you and it which shrinks until you actually can embrace it." "What the hell are you talking about?" I asked. "It's more than this heehaw music," she said. "You should try it, everyone should, especially now. It's never too late to try to understand." And just before she unmuted Garth Brooks on the screen: "Never too late to try to learn to love something or somebody you thought you hated."

Focus

She used to say, "Focus on the good." How corny. But today I take my mother's advice. The bad will be just fine without me. A neighbor waves as I haul out the garbage. A school bus delivers a father's precious package: the little girl steps off, he hugs her hard, she says, "Dad, you're smashing the cookies in my backpack." Later at the drug store the new worker not quite sure how to use the register, flustered, and the man in line says don't panic, take your time, he had the same job once, he knows those things could frustrate Einstein. The bad will be waiting. For now, bread wafting from the bread factory. My window open all the way. Radio off, life streams in with its beautiful chaos. "Let it wait," I can hear her say. Then back home. To have a home. To open the door. To see the kitchen where I will slice a tomato and add a sliver of mozzarella, then a leaf of basil, some olive oil. But first, to open the fridge and pull out a bottle. Uncork. Pour. The liquid, gold. To sip. To hear her voice: "Focus." So I do. The wine so cold. So crisp. To sit at the table. To take one bite. Then another. To leave the TV off. To watch through the window the tree's branch welcoming a bluebird.

Sure

Sure, she cleaned my clothes,
ironed, bathed me, fed me.
Sure, she taught me words,
this thing called God,
how to pray. Sure, she
packed lunches,
sewed on buttons, cheered
when I kicked a stupid ball.
Sure, she pinned my drawings
on the fridge, let me
help spread dough
with honey and nuts
then gave me the first
delicious bite of baklava. Sure,
she colored eggs with me
at Easter, coached the sign
of the cross. Sure,
after my divorce,
this old lady
drove me to a bar, bought me
a drink, had one herself
though she never drank. Sure,
she lived long,
so why these poems,
tears? Sure, she was
my mother and friend,
I thanked her now and then,
never enough, a typical son. Sure,
I wait for her to visit me in my dreams
because there's still this little boy inside
that refuses to say goodbye.

I Don't Know What to Call This

The old Greek lady I bump into
at the grocery, with her cane,
scolds me. Says my dead mother
wouldn't like that I haven't been to church
since she died.
     I don't tell her
about sitting every morning three hours
before sunrise, listening to silence.
How I make a stone of my body
and silence sometimes knocks
on me wanting to be let in. How I open
the smooth secret door
and greet it
and we study each other lovingly,
uncritical.
    I don't tell her
I believe silence is something
like God and my dead mother,
or part of her, but not exactly. Beyond
words. This small daily ritual
a kind of prayer, kind of church.
     She prays for me
when I'm awake and asleep, she watches
me, I'd better believe it, even now,
the lady says. "Be a good Greek boy
and make your mother happy," she smiles
as if I'm ten instead of fifty
with sore knees and high cholesterol.
     Then she hands me
a tomato, proceeds to reveal
her secret for picking the sweetest.
Thank you. I look down, examine the smooth
outer surface, perfect round orb,
blood-luscious red.

Breath of Venus

I keep a small bottle of her perfume.
Half-full.
What was left.
Her voice has faded.
And her scent.
Even parts of her face.
Like a ship moving farther out
to sea,
she is shrinking,
a speck,
no binoculars or telescope
help.
So I take it out.
Mini-sculpture.
Open the cap,
the top of Aphrodite's head.
Bring it to my nostrils.
Close my eyes.
Say hello.

My Father at 3 AM

I find him in my study sitting behind my desk. He flips through my notebooks. At first he seems startled. Like a deer ready to bolt. Maybe he's breaking a rule the dead have about leaving the living alone. I tell him it's ok, offer to make coffee. He starts to relax. We make small talk. I catch him up. Show him photos of his great grandson. He says he's still working to forget the things he loved to do. It takes years. Golfing. Grilling. Turning pages of a book. I ask about my mother. He says she's not sad. She knew it was her time. But she is just starting to learn to be dead. "Cut back on the drinking," he says, "it'll help with your sleep." And "More metaphors don't necessarily make a poem better." And "Love your wife." He cups my face with his hands. I look into his eyes, see through them like binoculars—far away my mother studying herself in a strange mirror. "She is working at it," he says. Then he's gone before I can ask about God, infinity, floating, and whatnot. So I go back to bed, hold Carole. Fall asleep curled around her, like a question mark.

Her Wind Chimes

Today I take them out of storage,
attach them to a beam above the front porch,
and wait.

All day they barely move,
but in the middle of the night
they won't stop.

She must feel bolder in the dark.

I stare at the ceiling.
Listen,
until the sun comes up.

Two Years Later

    Maybe I was meant to find it,

like a message in a bottle

    tossed by her into the roiling surf . . .

(going through a box in the attic I forgot was there)

    . . . as if to say the ocean is not so wide between us:

her brush from the hospital,

    and in the bristles a few strands of hair.

III.
The Afterlife

The Afterlife

Two boys found her on the beach
and started performing surgery,
popping out glassy eyes,
unscrewing the head.
Others noticed and huddled close
to watch. The boys let a little girl
with a striking resemblance
take the head and she sat
under an umbrella pulling a comb
through long blond hair.
A seagull swooped, plucked
an eyeball that rolled away.
The arms came off.
The boys stuck them in sand
so it looked as if
a buried person were clawing
her way up from deep
in the earth.
They threw legs back
and someone's dog dived into surf
fetching one, which made
everyone laugh.
Then the sun sank.
Nobody stayed.
Waves kept rolling.
All that remained was the torso
like a capsule or an ark,
which nobody wanted,
but soon small creatures
arrived, arm and leg sockets
round doors
for easy access and escape.

Between the Appetizers and the Entrees

Of course, I wasn't there,
no one was,
as the bullet spiraled
through the barrel
and corkscrewed
into your mouth.
The hole it left
in the back of your head
I imagine plugging
with my finger
like the little Dutch boy
plugging the leaky dam.
I would leave it there
holding the mess in
until we figured
something out.
Like Holland,
there would be a happy ending,
the you inside you intact.
But in this story
your family is drowning,
even if they pretend they're not.
Dead you sits
on your mother's shelf
in a vase.
During the tornado warning
she took you with her
to the basement, said
"I can't lose him again."
Your sister tells us
as she passes me the pepper
at the restaurant,
trying to laugh.

Urgent Prayer

    When I picked up,
the recorded voice said,
        "Press #1 for urgent prayer."

How could I have known
    that later that day
you'd murder you

        on your parents' patio?
Robocalls
    in the name of the Lord

are nothing new. I've heard
      of them.
But this was my first,

    and no other since.
I'm sorry
      I rolled my eyes,

sorry
    I hung up the phone.
Write it in blood.

    Write it
in stone.
    Whatever a you or me is

I pray for now
      in case some god
picks up,

    doesn't roll his eyes,
doesn't hang up,
      and listens.

The Stain on the Concrete

Never left.
Refused to be erased.
Faded but still blooms.
Like a pink rose
through cement.
Defied hours, days
of scrubbing
with sponges, detergents.
Stubborn,
as if to say
here.
Like a period
or exclamation mark.
Like a birthmark
on skin.
Deathmark
on stone.
We know it's there
under the throw rug
with tropical flowers.
We make small talk
and carefully step over it
with drinks in our hands.

The Woodpecker

He arrived yesterday,
landed on my sill.
He pecks his tiny sledgehammer
against the frame.
I open the window,
shoo him,
he flies away,
comes back a minute later.
Poe had his raven,
I have my woodpecker.

Is it you, Ryan, in a bird suit?
You were always stubborn.
Even after the accident,
even without a face,
you rode your Kawasaki,
arms and legs full of pins and metal.

Your parents drove you nuts.
You showed them who's boss.
Left them with a mess to clean up.
And nightmares.
Shouldn't you be pecking their house?

Are you marking your territory with sound?
Are you drilling a hole for a nest?
Or are you trying to say something?
What do you want?
Will this poem suffice?

If it's not you, just some bird,
you'd admire his sleek head,
his tenacity. His fierce desire.
All the trees in the woods
and he insists on this spot.
How foolish. How macho.

Online it says to use a visual
deterrent to rid him off.
Aluminum foil? A fake squirrel?
I'll let him peck a little longer.
Would that make you happy?
And by the way,
any chance you've seen my dead mother?

Self-Service

The abandoned gas station with rusted out pumps and weeds sprouting through cracks

    in concrete still has the sign in big yellow letters. If you drive by the perfect moment

    of dusk you might see ghosts who stop there not for gas or chips or beef jerky or beer,

but to bring themselves for their own repairs. They change the soul's oil,

check the heart's timing belt, rotate memory's tires. They still tinker, try to fix

    the springs and coils of their lives. Regrets, jealousies, angers, guilts

    keep them coming back. Who can blame them for wanting to make things right,

although you want to tell them they can trade in the old self for a new one.

They can leave the old self behind with its dents and wheezing engine, its damaged

    brakes. But you're no medium, no god. All you can do is watch as they impatiently wait

    their turns, lined up in the self-service aisle,
their milky bodies fading in and out.

Squid

Slimy aliens from another planet.

The Greek fisherman batters them against rocks.
Their brains and guts like snot.
Some play dead, I'm sure, but die anyway.
In a pile they look like empty gloves.

Forty odd years later

the waitress places the large platter
between us and the other couple, our friends,
no one with a clue I'm eight years old,
my adult body what they see

as they squeeze lemons, clink glasses.

I've eaten calamari a hundred times.
So why today am I yanked back to that beach
on Rhodes near that fisherman as my father
and mother, happy to be young again,

sit at an umbrella table,

sipping wine, now and then waving to me?
Maybe they were waiting and hoping,
wherever in oblivion,
that this miracle might happen.

That a moment like all moments slipping by

becoming what we call *the past*
could suddenly surface from time's ocean,
if even briefly, bringing them to a place
called *the present*, as they hold hands

a little longer, wondering how

this is even possible. To be breathing, undead,
looking into each other's eyes.
As the Greek fisherman smashes
the last bubble skulls on the rocks

and my wife and friends eat and drink and laugh.

Treasures

While other men golfed or took apart engines or watched football, Sunday afternoons my father would visit some cheap outlet store. He could go anywhere now. But he preferred to wander the country of dollar t-shirts, discounted CDs, bins of chocolate bars with no expirations. He'd go for hours, his relaxation, pick up and examine every item—gaudy paper weight, nail clippers, box of pencils—as if for the first time, amazed, and oh the prices! He'd leave with bags of something. A thousand popsicle sticks. Three hundred cardboard book marks. I'd sneak into his study, find cabinets crammed full. Only later I understood. How he grew up fatherless, so poor, in an Athens ghetto. How his yearly Christmas gift was an orange. How skinny he was. Even stealing nuts from a street cart. The little boy always inside him, stowed away, hiding when the man came to America must have whispered every Sunday how sad he still was. Probably poked and prodded from behind the ribs. Which would explain the cheapo knickknacks, no doubt the little boy's eyes spotted looking out of my father's eyes, big with excitement and glee at the miraculous lucky finds, the treasures.

Stethoscope

When, not feeling well,
she went to see
Dr. Rene Laennec
and he was embarrassed
to press his ear to her bosom
so he rolled paper into a tube
and listened to her heart
which he later improved with wood
which later evolved into headset,
acoustic ducts and ear pods,
how could the young woman have known
she would reach through centuries to here?
How could Laennec have known
he'd land in this poem
about a son whose father
was a doctor,
how home late from work
the father would peek
into the boy's room
as the boy fought sleep
then the boy would beg
to be examined
because he wanted his father
to linger, and even though
the father was exhausted
he would press the silver dollar-size
disc of glass
to the boy's chest
before a goodnight kiss?

How could anyone have predicted
on that day in 1816 France
that this invention, this thing
would be all the son has
of his father's now
when the father is dead,
and he sometimes takes it out
when he thinks of him,
and touches the disc of glass
like a small mouth
to his own cheek?

My Wife Taking Off Her Shirt

Her arms cross over her belly
as if she's hugging herself,
then she grabs the cotton fabric
at each hip, pulls it over her head
in one smooth motion,
the shirt inside-out rising like
a fountain shooting up
then her arms come back down,
the shirt in one hand
she lets drop to the floor
leaving her two naked breasts,
nipples looking
straight at me
just a second before
she slips on the sweatshirt
she likes best after a hard
day's work.

Is this one of a million fragments
that gets lost, glossed over
by other bigger chunks of
making love or weeping
or talking in the dark?
Not a birth, a death
or cataclysmic shift—
a single human crumb,
that again in some screening room
where I'll be forced to sit viewing
scenes I lived but wasn't fully
present for, it will be played back
and I'll protest, assert I was there,
I finally did *see* it that one day in
October around 6 p.m. on Earth,
and the projectionist will apologize,

"Yes, you did see that one, my mistake"
and the next scene will play.

The sweatshirt hangs down to her
creamy mid-thighs.
Her bare feet on hardwood.
She reaches behind her head
with both hands, pulls out
from inside the sweatshirt collar
long blond hair which spills
down in waves over her shoulders
to her waist. I drop the invisible
coins into the invisible slot
to pay attention.
Have I seen anything
so thrilling? She notices
me watching-not blinking.
"What are you thinking?" she asks.
I don't speak.
The room is quiet.
The quiet is trying to tell us something.
"What?" she says.

Stethoscope II

When I read her my tender, touching poem about my dead father's
stethoscope, how it is his only possession I own,
how it brings back sweet memories of him listening to my heart,
my wife reminds me of the time in an apartment
when I took it out to better hear through the wall
our neighbors having sex, yipping and howling,
the way I looked like a mad doctor pressing the glass disc
here and there, searching for the prime spot,
how she said "What would your father think if he could see this?"
but she also wanted to hear and did
then turned around facing me and said,
"Geeze, it's just their two kids squealing loud—
that's what you should write about."

Grandson

His eyes are too wise for a one year old. He doesn't blink as he gazes at me, as if he knows that I know he once was a Tibetan monk who spoke telepathically to the leaves, who lived alone on a mountain carving small wooden animals to give to poor children, who sipped tea and ate raw beans and chanted using incense . . .

*

I crawled through the open windows of his pupils, found myself inside a small hut. He brought out rice cookies. We sat on the floor. He sprinkled water on our heads. Showed me a flower petal he'd been studying for a hundred years. He refused to brush aside a fly that landed on his nose for fear of fracturing its delicate legs. He was full of compassion that had fermented for centuries. He even offered to show me other incarnations he was, all the way to when he lived as a dog that barked at birds and licked bare feet of sleeping beggars. But I said I'd better be going. So I crawled back out into the living room . . .

*

His mother holds him on her lap.
I bow to him.
He smiles at me, tranquilly.
Then he falls asleep.
Just like a little old man.

The Dream

It is a busy place.

Now and then you recognize somebody you know boarding or disembarking.

You might wave, or if there's time, even say something.

(My mother died just days before my daughter knew she was pregnant).

*

In the terminal my mother's soul arriving bumps into Brodie's leaving.

She asks if he's excited for the journey. "I'm your great grandmother." He nods.

She tells him about his soon-to-be mother, and his grandfather—me.

He asks where she's headed. She doesn't quite know.

*

There is not much time for chitchat.

"I hope it's nice," he says.

They understand they won't remember this.

They hug and move on. I wake. It is good to know they met, if even briefly.

Watching TV With Brodie

On the screen we watch cartoons. The Roadrunner *beep beeps* and the coyote scoots off the cliff yet hangs, his scrawny body running in air, not falling until he looks down, then lands on the canyon floor, making a puff of dust. He returns in the next frame, his flattened body springing back to shape.

The little boy is not yet two and I wonder if a grandfather's job is to teach a grandson death. The people who jumped out of the burning twin towers didn't spring back to shape or merely stand up, brushing dust off, a few animated stars swirling around their sore heads. They turned into puddles. Left craters where they landed.

He looks up at colorful animals who can talk. Bugs Bunny, fleeing rifle-toting Elmer Fudd, draws a door on a boulder, opens it, and passes through, leaving Elmer confused and muttering "Where is that pesky wabbit?!" Earlier on the same screen I watched breaking news of yet another school shooting. The gunman chased students who locked themselves in a closet and all he had to do was shoot through the door, which he did.

I watch the little boy's wide eyes. He grins. He doesn't really know what he's seeing. He will. Soon enough. But for now we sit on this comfy couch, a wool blanket over our laps, and we eat Cheerios one by one out of a blue bowl.

Random Love

Today a stranger said, "I love you." Said it looking right at me, a few feet away
    as he turned around before entering the store, although it was intended for

    the woman he thought was beside him who had stopped to adjust her shoe.
He was embarrassed but it was too late. He couldn't take them back. I wouldn't

give them back. The words were mine now, precious. I added them
    to my collection. Some people collect coins, stamps,

    shark teeth. I keep them in an echo chamber inside
my skull where I play them back whenever I want.

I've mostly snagged words of my mother and father and wife and children,
    but now and then something like this happens. You never know

    when you'll crave a stranger's love. So his words are in there, catalogued,
saved. He smiled and shrugged and said "I meant I love her," pointing

to the woman on the sidewalk. But words are birds
    sprung from a cage—once you say them, bye bye.

    He held the door open for me, and I smiled back as I passed through,
and I winked, and said, "I love you too."

Love Account

Like savings,
every month I deposit some
for future use.
I'm preparing just in case
one day I wake up empty,
a bitter, lonely man.
I don't want to come across
a puppy on a walk and curse no leash
instead of bending over to pat its furry head.
I don't want to curse my phone
when my children don't call.
Don't want to give the finger
to the mailbox, to the garbage men doing their job,
to my neighbor obsessed with cutting his grass.
That's why I put a little of my love aside.
I have to choose what to love completely,
what to love slightly less.
The full moon like a giant pearl, I love,
but can get away with about 63.5 percent.
My grandson's laugh is harder,
I strain to hold back, say, 10 percent.
I need to be able to stick my card into a slot
for the love I saved to come out.
You can't withdraw what isn't there.
I try to tell her.
But my wife says she wants 110 percent every day.

My friend is having a good week.
He eats as though making up for lost meals.
Downs forkfuls of lasagna,
grabs breadsticks he dunks in marinara.
He hardly pauses to speak,
nods his bald head
but he's not really listening.

He notices my eyes amazed, says
"I'm eating for two, me and my tumor."
We laugh.
I picture it inside him, a golf ball with a face,
mouth open wide like a baby bird in a nest.
He knows this doesn't make sense,
he should be starving it
but he'd be starving himself too.
I say "Maybe we should drown it,"
pour us more wine. We drink.
He says "I think it likes that too."
"Is it a boy or a girl? What will you name it?"
I ask. He grins. I grin.
He looks down at his plate, then up into my eyes,
says "Your wife is right, math is dumb"—
then with a bony hand he wipes his mouth
with a napkin, says "Spend it. Spend all of it."

Why I Like the Wind

Because it willingly collides with objects
to let us hear its voice.

Because it moves things to teach us
the invisible is real.

Because it never grew up,
never stays in one place, curious,
touches everything
and puts things in its mouth.

Because it picks up leaves
when we're not looking,
tries to reattach them
to a branch.

Because it believes
in what's impossible,
like a child,
which is why it loves children most,
follows them as they skip,
hovers as they pretend
in a sandbox.

Because it waits outside of windows,
impatient, as we sleep.

Because it gets bored easily,
messes up a woman's hair
for kicks.

Because it scatters dollar bills
a man drops to watch
him chase them
down a sidewalk.

Because no matter the weather,
it refuses
to end itself.

Because it laughs at us,
and weeps for us.

Because it uses my dead mother's wind chimes
to send me her messages.

Bargain

Somewhere in the womb
you signed the contract.
Let the shady figure without a face
wrap your tiny fingers around the pen.
Let him guide your hand
to the dotted line to mark
your real name—
the name even your parents never knew.
Now your heart breaks
over and over in this place.
The world's cruel machinery
makes sure of this.
People suffer, die, inexplicably.
It's too late.
You didn't read the fine print.
But then, sometimes it happens.
A single bird, like the hand
of a genius mathematician
holding a marker, darts back
and forth, figuring equations
on the whiteboard of the sky.
Driving, you pass a horse in a pasture
slipping its skin
to join the shadow of a tree.
On your block,
a man aims a garden hose at children
as sun through tree leaves
makes a sudden stained-glass window,
and they squeal and run and tumble
in their small electric bodies.

I Enter the Door

              and look out at
an old man
holding his feeble wife's hand
on a bench,
their walkers parked
beside them,
tiny brave sparrows
at their feet pecking at
bread crumbs the man scatters
with his free hand
as the spirit-thing inside the woman
smiles, which makes the outer
woman's mouth curl,
and the thing inside the man
sends the command to point
so the flesh and bone finger
points to a lone duck
waddling by,
and she leans and rests
her human head on his shoulder
and he turns his human head
and rests it on her head
as the sparrows in their feathered costumes
hop and peck and seem to do a little jig,
too busy or happy to care
how the unknowable inside the sun
directs the sun's rays to reach
from behind a cloud
anointing all of them.